CAPITAL

CAPITAL

LYNN CURLEE

Aladdin Paperbacks
New York London Toronto Sydney

It is a pure geometrical form, an immense unadorned tapering marble shaft as tall as a fifty-story skyscraper. The Washington Monument, built to honor the first president of the United States, stands at the heart of our nation's capital city, which was also named for the father of our country. The enormous obelisk is the centerpiece of a magnificent public space, a vast sweeping expanse of grass, trees, and water, surrounded by the bustling metropolis of Washington, D.C.

To the east, almost a mile and a half away, at the end of a broad promenade of lawns lined with rows of stately elm trees, the enormous bulk of the Capitol of the United States spreads across the crest of Capitol Hill. With its lofty gleaming white dome, the Capitol building dominates the capital city. It is the seat of government and the architectural symbol of America.

Facing north from the Monument, one may glimpse a beautiful estate, set like a jewel among the trees. Impressive, but also simple and gracious, the White House, once known as the "President's House," is the official residence and office of the president of the United States.

Turning to the west, at the end of a grand Reflecting Pool more than one-third of a mile long, a simple rectangular marble temple sits serenely on its podium. The Abraham Lincoln Memorial is a shrine to the sixteenth president, the great statesman who steered the United States through its most terrible conflict, the Civil War, and whose policies ended the shameful practice of slavery in America.

And to the south, across the Tidal Basin, a lovely body of water surrounded by Japanese cherry trees, stands the Thomas Jefferson Memorial. A graceful circular temple with its own small dome, it honors the third president, great intellect, and author of the Declaration of Independence, the document that states the basic philosophy upon which America was founded, the idea "that all men are created equal."

These five great structures—the U.S. Capitol, the White House, the Washington Monument, the Lincoln Memorial, and the Jefferson Memorial—are the major official focal points of the immense open space, the National Mall. A grand and beautiful public park built on a huge scale, the National Mall spans more than two miles, from the Capitol to the Lincoln Memorial. The streets surrounding the Mall are lined with monumental government buildings and great museums. Here are the National Gallery of Art and the various departments of the Smithsonian Institution, such as the National Museum of Natural History and the National Air and Space Museum. The Mall is also home to the National Archives, where the most precious documents of American civilization are kept: the Declaration of Independence, the U.S. Constitution, and the Bill of Rights. Here also are smaller, more intimate memorials and monuments, such as the Vietnam Veterans Memorial, the Korean War Veterans Memorial, and the Franklin Delano Roosevelt Memorial, honoring the thirty-second president. Center of government and culture, popular tourist attraction, and one of the most spectacular ceremonial spaces on earth, the National Mall is the symbolic heart of the United States of America.

The city of Washington, District of Columbia, was founded by President George Washington himself. During the years after the end of the American Revolution in 1783, the government of the new nation had moved from city to city, having no permanent home. But the Constitution,

THE FEDERAL CITY

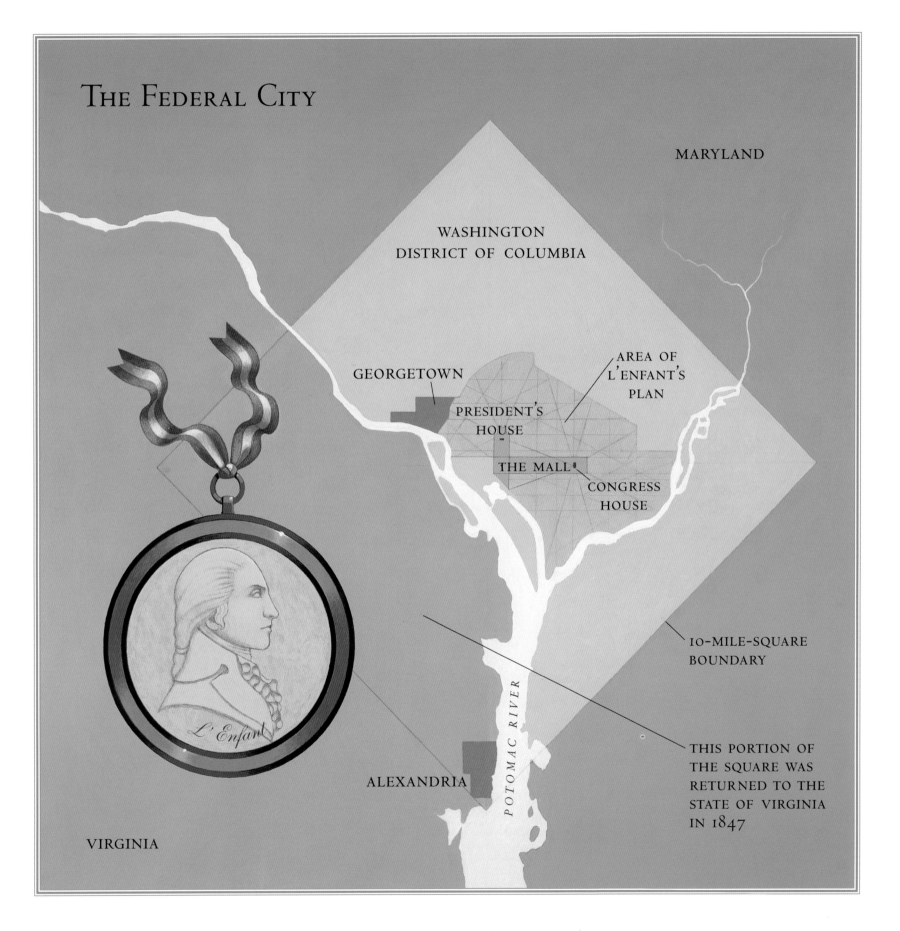

MARYLAND

WASHINGTON
DISTRICT OF COLUMBIA

AREA OF
L'ENFANT'S
PLAN

GEORGETOWN

PRESIDENT'S
HOUSE

THE MALL

CONGRESS
HOUSE

10-MILE-SQUARE
BOUNDARY

POTOMAC RIVER

ALEXANDRIA

THIS PORTION OF
THE SQUARE WAS
RETURNED TO THE
STATE OF VIRGINIA
IN 1847

VIRGINIA

L'Enfant

written in 1787, authorized a new capital city to be built in a federal district that would belong to no state, but to the entire country. In 1790, in a compromise worked out between the northern and southern states, the First Congress decided that the new capital would be built on the banks of the Potomac River, which flows between Maryland and Virginia.

President Washington was given the privilege of personally choosing the exact location, acquiring the land, and developing it for the nation. He chose a site on the river, a landscape of wetlands, small hills, pastures, and orchards between the prosperous communities of Alexandria, Virginia, and Georgetown, Maryland, and near to his home, Mount Vernon, Virginia.

The president appointed engineer and architect Major Pierre-Charles L'Enfant to develop an overall plan for the new city. Born and educated in France, L'Enfant had come to America in 1776 as a young man to fight in the Revolution. He was drawn by the ideals of liberty and equality, and he loved his adopted country passionately. He vowed to create a capital "magnificent enough to grace a great nation."

The Constitution stated that the new city should not exceed "10 miles square." L'Enfant envisioned a rectangular grid of streets within that square. Superimposed on the grid were broad avenues radiating diagonally from the major official buildings, the "Congress House" and the "President's Palace." This plan provided numerous squares, circles, and triangles at street intersections where monuments and fountains could be placed, with the broad avenues providing grand vistas between them.

The president and L'Enfant chose Jenkins Hill, a rise about 90 feet above the Potomac, as the site for the Congress House, or the Capitol. L'Enfant called the hill "a pedestal waiting for a monument."

The President's House (Washington refused to call it a palace) would be built in an existing orchard about a mile and a half to the northwest, and it would connect with the Capitol by one

of the broad radiating avenues. L'Enfant's plan also provided a site for a monumental equestrian statue of George Washington, as the great Revolutionary War general, on a small knoll directly south of the President's House and due west of Jenkins Hill. Between the Capitol and the statue, L'Enfant planned a magnificent boulevard 400 feet wide, to be lined with gardens, town houses, and sloping lawns. He called it "the Mall." Pierre L'Enfant designed the capital city of the small new nation for posterity. He made it "on a scale fit for a vast empire."

Although a brilliant urban designer, L'Enfant was also imperious and egotistical. He was unable to compromise with other government officials to get things done. Regrettably, the president had to remove him from his position, but L'Enfant's plan for the capital of the United States had fired the imaginations of Washington and Jefferson, and today it exists much as he envisioned it, but on an even vaster scale.

In 1792, as soon as the site was surveyed and the major thoroughfares planned, two architectural competitions were held, one for the Capitol and one for the President's House. The commission for the Capitol was won by Dr. William Thornton, physician and amateur architect. His plan called for a large classical structure in three parts: a central rotunda with two wings, one for each House of Congress. The rotunda was to be topped by a hemispherical dome. Dr. Thornton's design was enthusiastically endorsed by George Washington and Thomas Jefferson. The classical style of architecture was considered particularly appropriate by the founding fathers. They believed that they were reviving noble political ideals invented by the ancient Greeks and Romans, and they wanted a capital city that would recall the spirit of Athens and the early Roman republic.

The competition for the President's House was won by James Hoban, an architect and builder originally from Ireland, who designed the mansion in the style of an Irish country estate. His plan was adopted over that of Thomas Jefferson, who had entered the competition anonymously.

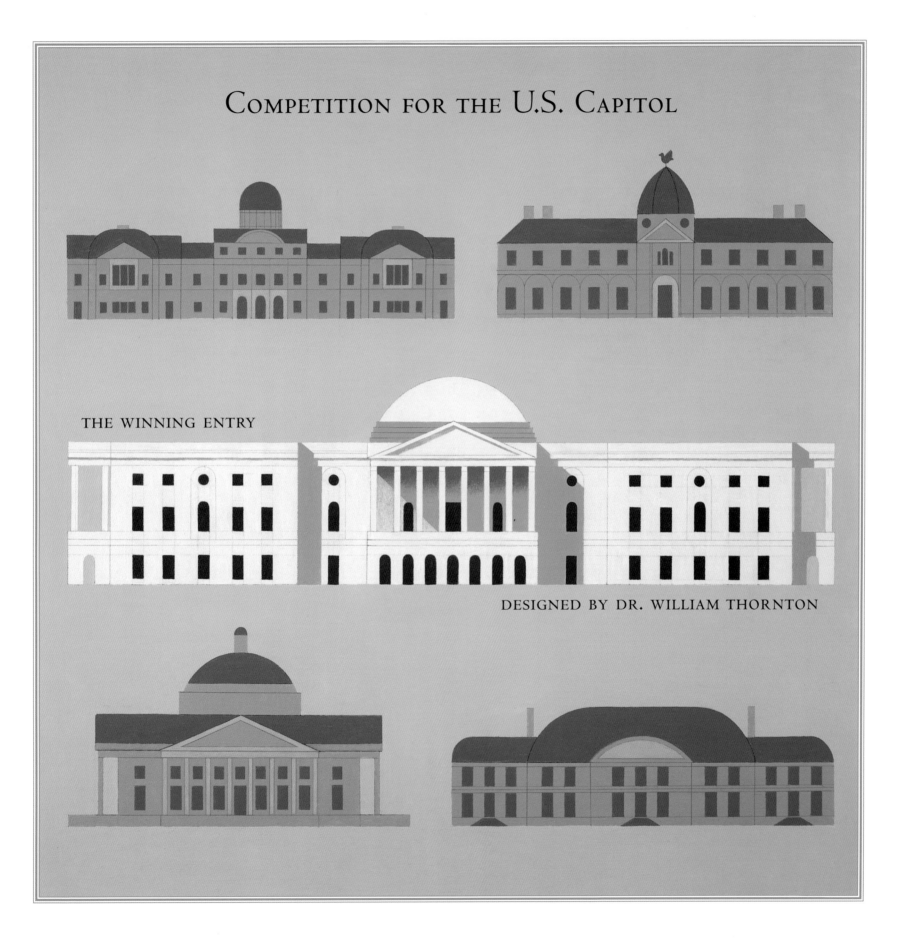

COMPETITION FOR THE U.S. CAPITOL

THE WINNING ENTRY

DESIGNED BY DR. WILLIAM THORNTON

The Capitol was begun immediately. The cornerstone of the U.S. Capitol building was laid personally by President Washington in an elaborate ceremony on September 18, 1793. The mansion was begun a year later.

In 1799, George Washington died. He had declined to run for a third term of office in 1796, and his vice president, John Adams, had been elected to succeed him. By the turn of the century construction of the first phase of the Capitol, its North Wing, was finished and the President's House was nearly complete. President Adams therefore ordered the move to the federal city, and the executive offices of the United States opened in Washington, D.C., on June 15, 1800. Congress first convened in the new seat of government five months later. At the beginning of a new century, the new nation now had a new capital.

The city grew slowly and haphazardly along L'Enfant's grand avenues. Most people disliked Washington, D.C. They lived there only because they had to. At first a very small settlement with only a couple of large buildings under construction, it was raw, isolated, and provincial. But gradually town houses and businesses were built and the government settled into its new home.

Then came the War of 1812. On August 24, 1814, a British raiding party torched the capital of the United States. The Capitol, the President's House, and many other buildings were gutted by fire and left as smoking ruins. Only a violent storm with driving rain that quenched the flames prevented them from being completely destroyed. Many felt that now the capital should be moved to a proper city, but cooler heads prevailed, maintaining that rebuilding in the same place would be symbolic of winning the war. In 1815 the rebuilding of the nation's capital began. The government met in temporary quarters until it was completed.

". . . the first temple dedicated to the sovereignty of the people."
—Thomas Jefferson

When the British burned Washington, the Capitol of the United
States was still not finished. The South Wing had been constructed between 1803 and 1807 by
Benjamin Henry Latrobe, appointed surveyor of public buildings by President Thomas Jefferson.
Latrobe had emigrated from England in 1795, and he was the first true professional architect-engineer
in America. Educated in the classical tradition, Latrobe made changes in Dr. Thornton's interior
plans to make the South Wing more useful, and he reconstructed parts of the North Wing as well,
adding a chamber for the Supreme Court. By 1811, Latrobe's work on both wings was finished,
and they were joined by a temporary wooden arcade. This was the building that the British burned.

After the war, in 1815, Latrobe began to rebuild the Capitol, which he called "a most magnificent
ruin." He took the opportunity to redesign parts of the gutted interiors. He also enriched the building
with classical details and embellishments, such as his famous interior column capitals, carved with
tobacco leaves and corn plants. Latrobe resigned in 1817 when disputes about construction delays
and labor costs arose. He was replaced by Charles Bulfinch, a prominent Boston architect. Bulfinch
finished rebuilding the chambers for the Senate, the House of Representatives, and the Supreme
Court in 1819. He then turned to the construction of the rotunda and the dome. Against Bulfinch's
advice, it was the idea of President James Monroe to make the copper-clad wooden dome somewhat
taller than Dr. Thornton's original hemispherical design. The work was done by 1826, and the
western terraces and landscaping were finished in 1829. Thirty-six years after the cornerstone was
laid by George Washington, the Capitol of the United States was complete.

Yet only twenty years later the building was bursting at the seams. By the mid-nineteenth century there were thirty states in the Union, and it was still growing rapidly. Both Houses of Congress had completely outgrown their chambers, and in 1850 an architectural competition was held for the enlargement of the Capitol. Congress was unable to decide the winner, so the prize of $500 was divided among five architects. The thirteenth president, Millard Fillmore, made the decision, choosing the design of architect-engineer Thomas Ustick Walter of Philadelphia.

Walter enlarged the Capitol by building two enormous extensions, one on the North Wing for the Senate and one on the South Wing for the House of Representatives. Faced with marble and decorated in grand classical style, each extension is almost as large as the entire original building. Since the extensions completely changed the proportions and scale of the structure, Walter provided plans to replace the wood and copper dome with something far more impressive and magnificent, and in 1855, Congress approved the construction of an immense new dome, more than twice the height of the original one.

Work progressed rapidly. In 1856 the old dome was removed and the new one was begun. By 1857 the South Extension was complete enough for the House of Representatives to meet in its new chamber, and in 1859 the Senate moved into the North Extension. All of this construction activity took place at a time of rising tensions between the northern and southern states over the issue of slavery, and in 1861 the nation exploded into civil war. In its geographical position between North and South, Washington, D.C., became an armed camp.

"Capitol Hill, dreary, desolate and dirty, stretched away into an uninhabited desert high above the mud of the West End. Arid hill and sodden plain showed alike the horrid trail of war." Troops were mustered in the city streets. Horses were corralled everywhere. The Washington Monument grounds were taken over for cattle pens and a slaughterhouse. Union officers commandeered

private homes for quarters. Churches, assembly halls, and mansions were filled with the wounded and dying of the American armies. And so was the Capitol. For a year at the beginning of the war, the great building itself became a hospital. But President Abraham Lincoln ordered that construction of the new dome continue: "If people see the Capitol going on . . . it is a sign we intend the Union shall go on."

On December 2, 1863, in the midst of war, an enormous crowd gathered to witness the placement of a monumental bronze Statue of Freedom atop the lantern of the newly completed dome. At noon a battery of thirty-five guns fired the national salute. The statue was sculpted in Rome by American artist Thomas Crawford. Freedom wears a helmet encircled with stars and capped with an eagle's head and feathers. She is almost 20 feet high and weighs over 7 tons. In her left hand she holds a wreath and shield, and her right hand rests on the hilt of her sword. Crawford sent the plaster model of the enormous figure from Rome by ship in 1858. The statue was cast in bronze and placed in storage until the dome was ready to receive it.

Walter's Capitol dome is a masterpiece of engineering, design, and symbolism. It is constructed of cast iron, the most modern and advanced building material available in the 1850s. Every part of the dome's structure was manufactured in a foundry, lifted into position by steam-powered derricks, and bolted into place. An inner shell is connected to the larger outer dome by trusses and girders. At about 9 million pounds, the ironwork is still far lighter than a masonry dome and could be assembled much faster.

For his design Walter drew upon the great European tradition of dome building. But the Capitol dome is utterly unique. The drum from which it springs has a ring of thirty-six columns, representing the number of states at the time, and the topmost lantern has thirteen columns, representing the thirteen original colonies. Painted a dazzling white, and with its noble profile, large

windows, and lofty height (288 feet above the ground), the Capitol dome is instantly recognizable. Triumphantly completed during the nation's most terrible crisis, the great dome came to symbolize the Union itself.

When the Civil War was over, the Capitol of the United States looked almost exactly as it does today. During the late nineteenth century Capitol Hill was re-landscaped and its terraces, facing the Mall, were reworked. This grand project was designed by Frederick Law Olmsted, the great landscape architect, who was also the creative genius behind New York City's Central Park. Of course, in almost a century and a half, the Capitol has been upgraded with plumbing, heating, electricity, elevators, air-conditioning, security devices, telephone and computer systems —all of the necessities and conveniences of modern life. In the late 1950s, to provide more interior room, the East Front of the Capitol was extended out by about 32 feet. The sandstone facades of the old North and South Wings designed by Dr. Thornton were reproduced in marble, and the original exterior walls were preserved inside the new addition.

The U.S. Capitol has been built, burned, rebuilt, domed, enlarged, redomed, extended, decorated, restored, redecorated, and restored again. It is has been called "quirky," "wasteful of space," and "ostentatious." But as one critic said, "One might as well object to extraneous features in the contours of the Grand Canyon or question a turn in the sweeping course of Niagara Falls as suggest that an ornament is out of order on the Capitol's vast white cliffs and noble summit. It is confirmation in rock that the whole is greater than the sum of its parts."

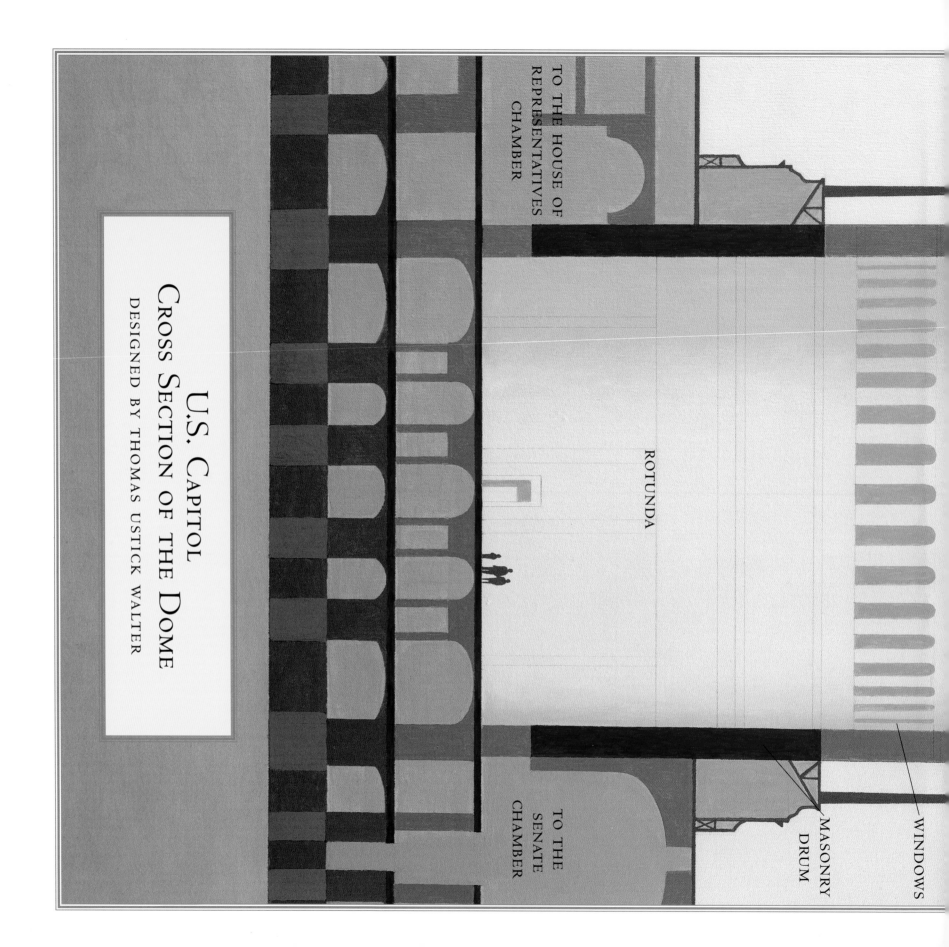

U.S. Capitol
Cross Section of the Dome
DESIGNED BY THOMAS USTICK WALTER

TO THE HOUSE OF REPRESENTATIVES CHAMBER

ROTUNDA

TO THE SENATE CHAMBER

MASONRY DRUM

WINDOWS

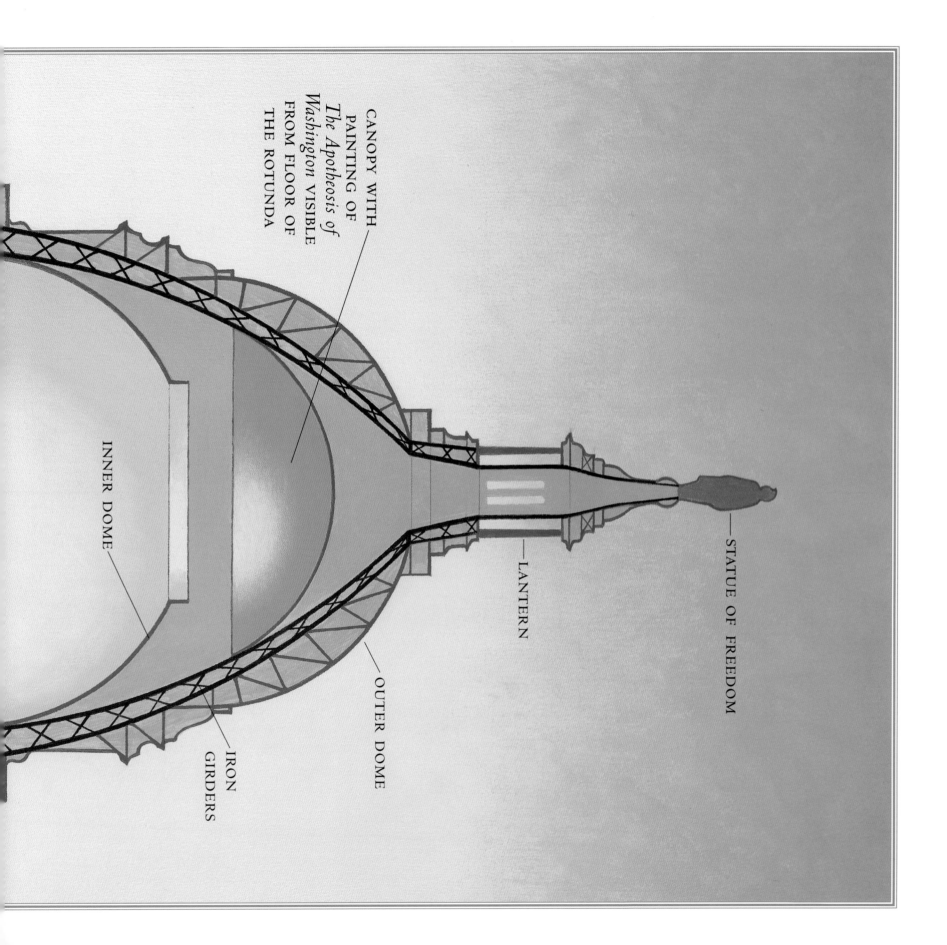

CANOPY WITH
PAINTING OF
*The Apotheosis of
Washington* VISIBLE
FROM FLOOR OF
THE ROTUNDA

INNER DOME

IRON
GIRDERS

OUTER DOME

LANTERN

STATUE OF FREEDOM

"The Palace . . . should stand in the Heart of a City."
—Leone Battista Alberti

When President John Adams moved his family to Washington in 1800, the President's House was almost, but not quite, done. According to Abigail Adams, the First Lady, "The house is made habitable but there is not a single apartment finished. . . .We have not the least fence, yard, or other convenience, without, and the great unfinished audience room I make a drying room of, to hang the clothes up in."

James Hoban, the architect, had designed a large, gracious, and comfortable mansion that was quite grand by the standards of eighteenth-century America. Critics, however, claimed it was "big enough for two emperors, one Pope, and the Grand Lama." Thomas Jefferson, a talented gentleman-architect in his own right, had lost the competition for its design. But when he became president in 1801, he seized the opportunity to make it more to his liking. He collaborated with Benjamin Latrobe, who was working on the Capitol, to make it more useful by adding terrace pavilions on the sides for stables and storage. President Jefferson was famous for his informality. He refused to be bound by the rigid rules of protocol, eliminating formal receptions and even greeting important guests in his riding clothes or his dressing gown. Most of his important work was done by writing letters, comfortably seated at a desk, his pet mockingbird perched on his shoulder.

Just when it seemed that the President's House was complete, disaster struck. The fire set by the British in 1814 completely destroyed the interior of the mansion. Only a portrait of George Washington and some silver were saved. The name "White House" dates from this early period. It has been suggested that when the interior was rebuilt after the war, the building's sandstone facades were first given a coat of white paint to hide the scorch marks from the fire, but it seems that people called it the White House even before that event. During the nineteenth century the official name was the "Executive Mansion," but in 1901, President Theodore Roosevelt proposed a change, and the White House became the official, as well as the popular, name of the president's home.

During the 1820s, James Hoban, influenced by the ideas of Jefferson and the drawings of Latrobe, built two great columned porticoes. The North Portico serves as the main carriage entrance, and the semicircular South Portico looks out over the gardens and the South Lawn. The two low colonnaded galleries extend out from each side of the mansion, with terraces planted as formal gardens on top. In 1902 the New York architectural firm of McKim, Mead, and White remodeled the interior of the mansion and added a large office wing on the west grounds.

The White House is surrounded by President's Park, 18 private acres of beautiful gardens and lawns, with groves of historical specimen trees representing eighty varieties, planted over the decades by different presidents and their families. During the administration of President Harry Truman, in the late 1940s, a second-floor porch was built into the South Portico, finishing the exterior of the White House as we see it today. But while Truman was president, it was also discovered that the internal wooden structure was in danger of deteriorating. One day the president's daughter Margaret was startled when a leg of her piano actually crashed through the floorboards. Since the building was structurally unsound, the decision was made to completely gut the White House and to rebuild the entire interior from the basement up with a steel framework. The new interior structure was designed to be more efficient, useful, and modern, but a lot of history was discarded. The exterior sandstone walls of James Hoban's President's House are all that remain of the original structure.

In the decades since the rebuilding, the White House has continued to be upgraded and modernized. Today it possesses all of the amenities necessary and appropriate for living comfortably and for conducting the business of America's head of state. Since it is an actual residence as well as an official building, the White House has always reflected the taste of the First Family in harmony with its historic architecture. During the Theodore Roosevelt era, at the turn of the twentieth century, for example, the State Dining Room was decorated in the style of the time with dark paneling, Flemish tapestries, palm plants, and stuffed big-game animal trophies.

Of course, as the residence of the most important person in town, the White House has always been the center of Washington society. And the city in the heart of which it stands is a far cry from that of 1842 as described by Charles Dickens, the great English novelist: "spacious avenues that begin in nothing and lead nowhere; streets a mile long that want only houses, roads and inhabitants; public buildings that need but a public to be complete; and ornaments of great thoroughfares which only need great thoroughfares to ornament."

Today Washington, D.C., is a great metropolis, and the White House has the qualities that L'Enfant wanted in the President's House: "the sumptuousness of a palace, and the agreeableness of a country seat." In recent decades the mansion has become a museum of traditional American style. It is a treasure trove of antiques, most of which are historically important. Beginning with First Lady Jacqueline Kennedy in the early 1960s, great efforts have been made to find wonderful pieces of furniture and accessories that were used by former presidents and their families and to return them to their rightful place of honor in "the people's house."

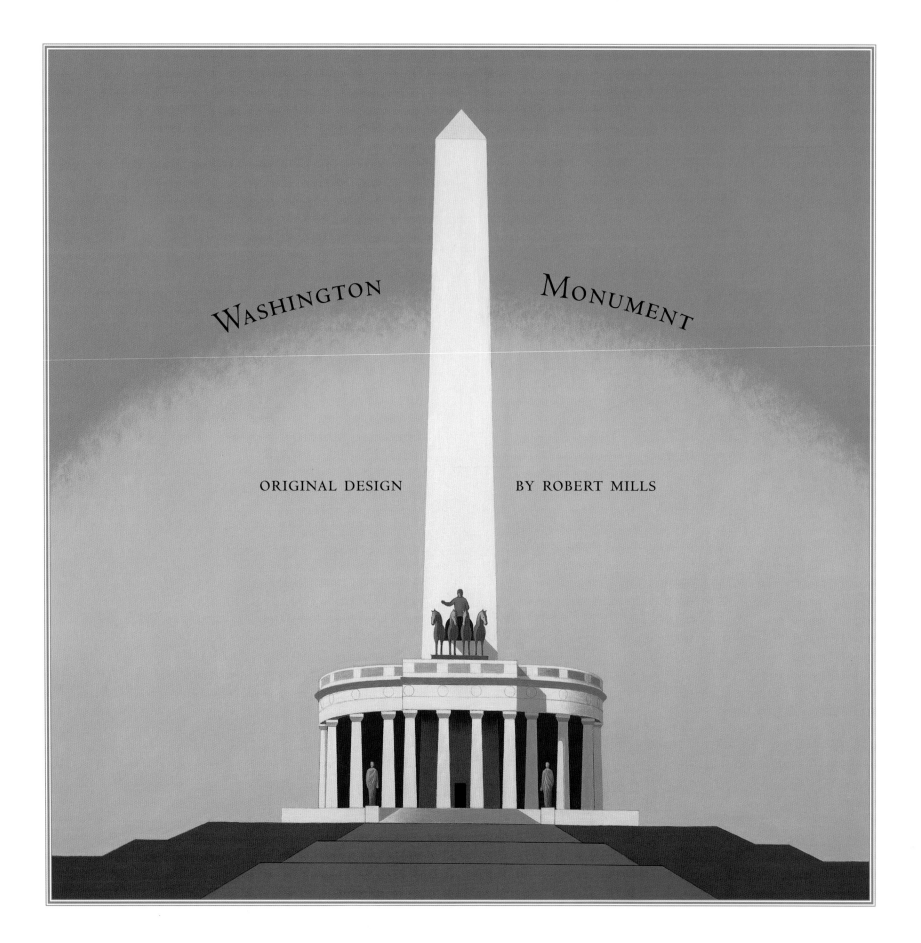

WASHINGTON MONUMENT

ORIGINAL DESIGN BY ROBERT MILLS

"First in war, first in peace, and first in the hearts of his countrymen."
—Henry Lee

George Washington had been the triumphant general of the Revolutionary War, and he was certainly the most charismatic statesman of his time. He was not a great intellect or a gifted orator, but he was a natural leader; and as the first president, his solid and modest personality and his careful policies were crucial to the success of the new nation. L'Enfant's plan had provided for an equestrian statue to be erected in his honor, but Washington himself had objected, and the matter was dropped.

After his death in 1799, the idea of honoring him was revived, but it was not until 1832 that the Washington National Monument Society was formed for the purpose of building a memorial in the capital city. The competition for its design was won by Robert Mills, another classically trained architect. Mills planned an immense tapering hollow obelisk made of cut stone blocks and surrounded by a circular colonnade adorned with several groups of statues. It was to be erected on the spot that L'Enfant had proposed for an equestrian monument. When ground was broken, it was discovered that the structure needed to be sited about 100 yards to the southeast to assure a more stable foundation. On July 4, 1848, the cornerstone of the Washington Monument was laid using the same trowel that George Washington himself had used for the Capitol's cornerstone ceremony.

Construction proceeded very slowly due to lack of funds. When the state of Alabama proposed donating an actual marble block instead of money, the plan was adopted, and building stones were accepted from states, territories, cities, organizations, and foreign nations. Built into the interior walls of the obelisk, these stones with their inscriptions may be seen today.

By the late 1850s the Monument had reached a height of 150 feet, but when the Civil War broke out, the project was halted, and the structure stood sadly as an unfinished stub for about twenty years. When work resumed in 1876, it was discovered that the Monument had tilted slightly. A new slab of concrete nearly 14 feet thick was laid under the old foundation before construction could continue. The place where building resumed may be seen clearly today because the original marble could not be matched precisely. At this point Mills's design was simplified. The fussy colonnade and statues were eliminated, and the proportions were changed to those of a traditional Egyptian obelisk.

On December 6, 1884, the topmost stone, a capstone weighing 3,300 pounds, was set during a howling gale. Its small flat upper surface was tipped with a small pyramid of solid aluminum. After the installation of 898 steps and a steam-powered elevator (a brand-new invention), the Monument was opened to the public on October 9, 1888. Over the decades, as technology has changed, the elevator has been upgraded and modernized several times, and the stonework has been cleaned and restored more than once.

For a few years, until the construction of the cast-iron Eiffel Tower in Paris in 1889, the Washington Monument was the tallest man-made object in the world. At 555 1/2 feet, it is still the tallest stone structure ever built and is almost twice as tall as the Capitol. Visible for many miles around, the starkly simple Monument makes a towering and magnificent centerpiece for the National Mall and a fitting memorial to the first president.

During the nineteenth century, as the city of Washington, D.C., grew around it, the Mall itself was neglected. The Smithsonian Institution's "Castle" was built infringing upon the Mall in 1847, and by 1875, L'Enfant's "Grand Avenue" was crisscrossed by roads and railroad tracks, with an enormous ornate Victorian railroad station almost in front of the Capitol. There were meandering pathways and clusters of trees. There was even a polluted canal, dug to help control flooding. The original vision for the center of the federal district was in danger of being lost. By the late 1890s "there was dismay among a number of prominent citizens over the increasingly shoddy appearance of the Capital City."

In 1901 a Senate commission was appointed by Congress to study the problem. Led by Senator James McMillan of Michigan, its members included two architects, a sculptor, and the son of America's leading landscape architect, Frederick Law Olmsted, who had recently designed the Capitol grounds. In its report the McMillan Commission recommended returning to the basic concepts of L'Enfant's original plan and stated that "departures from that plan are to be regretted and whenever possible remedied."

In the decades following, the train station on the Mall was torn down and the tracks removed. A grand new train station was built in the classical style. Union station is just a few blocks north of the Capitol. The Mall was cleared and planted with rows of trees. Space was reserved for monumental museum buildings to line the Mall near the Capitol. Previously the swampy wetlands west of the Washington Monument grounds were drained and the land reclaimed with landfill. The Mall was then extended beyond the Washington Monument nearly a mile to the new shoreline, and plans were made for a graceful stone bridge spanning the Potomac to Virginia. To the south, a riverside park was built around the lovely Tidal Basin.

". . . Government of the People, by the People, for the People . . ."
—Abraham Lincoln

George Washington seems remote to us, but we have photographs of Abraham Lincoln. We can look into his eyes and see the effects of the Civil War in his face. Rail-splitter, country lawyer, orator, president, commander in chief, murdered martyr, Great Emancipator—Lincoln is the most mythic figure in American history.

Two years after his assassination Congress appointed a commission to study the idea of a memorial to the sixteenth president, but its form and location were argued about for years. The solution was suggested by the McMillan Commission's report and made official in 1911. The western end of the newly extended Mall was finally chosen as the site for a monument to the man most considered to be the greatest president.

Architect Henry Bacon designed a beautiful marble temple based partly on the famous Parthenon in Athens. He added a tall rectangular attic story on top and placed the temple on a podium 14 feet high. A traditional Greek temple has the entrance at the end, but Bacon turned Lincoln's commemorative building so that the entrance is in the center of a long side facing the Capitol, more than 2 miles away. It is approached by a broad flight of steps leading up from the end of the 2,000 foot-long Reflecting Pool. There are thirty-six massive fluted Doric columns surrounding the building, representing the number of states at the time of Lincoln's death. On the parapet of the attic are carved forty-eight festoons, one for each state at the time the Memorial was built. The monument was dedicated on Memorial Day, May 30, 1922.

The interior is divided into three chambers. At the rear of the main room, facing the entrance, is a monumental statue of Abraham Lincoln, by Daniel Chester French. The sculptor's commission called for a statue 10 feet high, but when French tried his first model of the statue in the imposing space of the newly erected monument, he decided at once to enlarge the figure to heroic proportions. Lincoln is 19 feet high, seated in an enormous chair that is raised on a lofty podium. One hand is clenched and the other is relaxed. He sits looking sternly but with an expression of compassion toward the Washington Monument and the distant Capitol. The magnificent statue is made of twenty-eight blocks of gleaming white marble so perfectly joined that it seems to be carved from one huge block. French took a great deal of care to light the figure. During the day light filters through the translucent marble ceilings and pours through the entrance portal. At night spotlights dramatically illuminate Lincoln's craggy face with shining highlights and deep shadows.

Lofty columns separate the main room from the side chambers. High on their walls are subdued paintings of figures symbolizing Lincoln's ideals and philosophy, but the focal point of each side chamber is an enormous plaque carved with one of Lincoln's eloquent speeches. The noble and heartfelt words of the Gettysburg Address and the Second Inaugural Address are offered for contemplation: "With malice toward none, with charity for all."

Many visitors are profoundly moved by the Lincoln Memorial. Its architecture is severe, its mood grave and somber. Here we seem to be at the heart of America's conscience. If our nation has a soul, this is one place where it may be felt. The monument, its broad flight of steps, and the great length of the Reflecting Pool create a grand amphitheater that has been a place of protest and celebration since they were built. Here, most famously, Martin Luther King Jr. made a speech in which he challenged America to fulfill its ultimate promise as a place where everyone has an equal opportunity. "I have a dream," he proclaimed, with the statue of Abraham Lincoln looking over his shoulder.

"God who gave us life gave us liberty."
—Thomas Jefferson

In 1934, Congress authorized the construction of a memorial to Thomas Jefferson. But the greatest monument to the third president already existed. The Declaration of Independence was written in 1776 by a committee of enlightened patriots, but the words, the style, the cadences, the exact turns of phrase belong to Jefferson. Besides shaping words, Jefferson was also a shaper of buildings. His favorite form was the dome.

For his memorial, New York architect John Russell Pope designed a circular columned temple with an entrance portico and a beautiful dome. It recalls the Pantheon in Rome, the most famous domed building of the ancient world. Completed in the midst of World War II, the Jefferson Memorial was dedicated on April 13, 1943, the two-hundredth anniversary of his birth.

After the severe gravity of the Lincoln Memorial, the monument to Jefferson seems particularly graceful and serene in its lovely setting of circular terraces beside the Tidal Basin, especially when framed by a spectacular display of blossoming Japanese cherry trees every spring.

Located directly south of the White House and in line with the Washington Monument grounds, the Jefferson Memorial completes and defines a great cross-axis, at right angles to the Mall itself. From the South Portico of the White House, the president can look directly toward the statue of Thomas Jefferson, which stands about a mile away in the center of the Memorial. Rudulph Evans was the sculptor of the heroic bronze statue. It dominates the marble rotunda, which is open to the air on four sides. Panels are inscribed with significant passages from Jefferson's writings, and under the dome a circular frieze is carved with his stirring words, "I have sworn on the altar of God, eternal hostility to every form of tyranny over the mind of Man."

". . . the land of the free and the home of the brave."
—Francis Scott Key

By the mid-twentieth century, with the construction of the Jefferson Memorial completed, the overall design of the National Mall and its adjoining parks was set. The extension of the Mall to the west and the creation of the grand cross-axis with the Washington Monument at its core gave America a symbolic center on a magnificent scale far beyond even L'Enfant's dreams.

In the 1970s the Mall was cleared of the last of the temporary buildings that had marred its intended beauty. New museums lining the Mall are no longer built in the classical style, but they are beautifully made modern structures by some of the greatest architects of our age. Ignored and neglected in the nineteenth century, the National Mall is now considered one of our greatest treasures, and its space is zealously maintained and guarded. In the years since World War II, only a few memorials and monuments have been built in the vicinity of the Mall. The most celebrated of these is the Vietnam Veterans Memorial, a profoundly moving tribute to the dead of a controversial war that divided the nation.

World War II, however, was not controversial. It was a victory of freedom over tyranny. Now, at the beginning of the twenty-first century, a new memorial will take its place at our nation's heart on the main axis of the National Mall to commemorate the sacrifice and celebrate the victory of World War II, the most terrible and horrifying conflict in human history and the central event of the twentieth century. To locate this memorial on the main axis of the Mall is the highest possible honor for an entire generation of Americans. Built around the Rainbow Pool, the fountain located at the end of the Reflecting Pool near the Washington Monument, the World War II Memorial Plaza offers a place for contemplation, with its sweeping view of the National Mall, from the majestic Lincoln Memorial to the lofty gleaming Capitol dome in the distance.

The beautiful dome could have been destroyed during the terrorist attacks of September 11, 2001. For the first time in nearly two centuries, since the British burned Washington in 1814, our nation's capital was attacked by an enemy. The Pentagon was deliberately struck by an airplane, and apparently the White House and the Capitol were primary targets, but to the relief of all Americans, this part of the terrorists' plot did not succeed. Our Capitol building still dominates our capital city.

Planned so long ago, the National Mall is a world-famous destination visited by millions of tourists every year. It is the site of national holiday celebrations, concerts, and fireworks displays. It is a public park offering opportunities for recreation in the middle of a great city. And it is the place where great numbers of people can assemble in a peaceful way to let their opinions be known to the government.

The Mall is an open-air museum of U.S. history and a shrine to the promise of America, and it is open to everyone. And the great monuments that define it have always been open to the public as well. Everyone can enter the Capitol, that grand old building with two hundred years of history built into it. Everyone can walk its famous halls, or visit the chambers where the business of our government is done, or stand in the vast echoing rotunda and look up inside the great dome. Everyone can visit the White House for a tour of the public spaces. Everyone can ride the elevator to the top of the Washington Monument and take in the breathtaking view of the nation's capital. And everyone can climb the broad steps of the Lincoln and Jefferson Memorials and read the inspiring words of great men carved in stone and think about who we have been, who we are, and who we might become.

"We shape our buildings and afterwards our buildings shape us."
—Winston Churchill

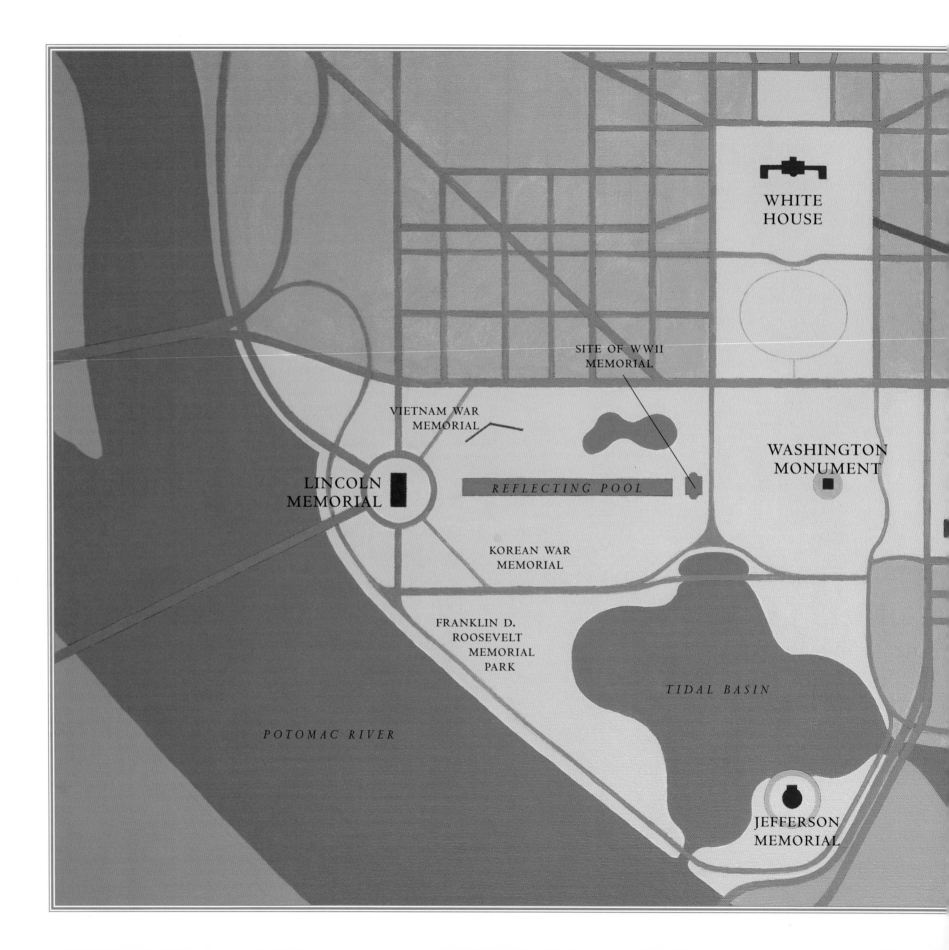

WHITE
HOUSE

SITE OF WWII
MEMORIAL

VIETNAM WAR
MEMORIAL

LINCOLN
MEMORIAL

REFLECTING POOL

WASHINGTON
MONUMENT

KOREAN WAR
MEMORIAL

FRANKLIN D.
ROOSEVELT
MEMORIAL
PARK

TIDAL BASIN

POTOMAC RIVER

JEFFERSON
MEMORIAL

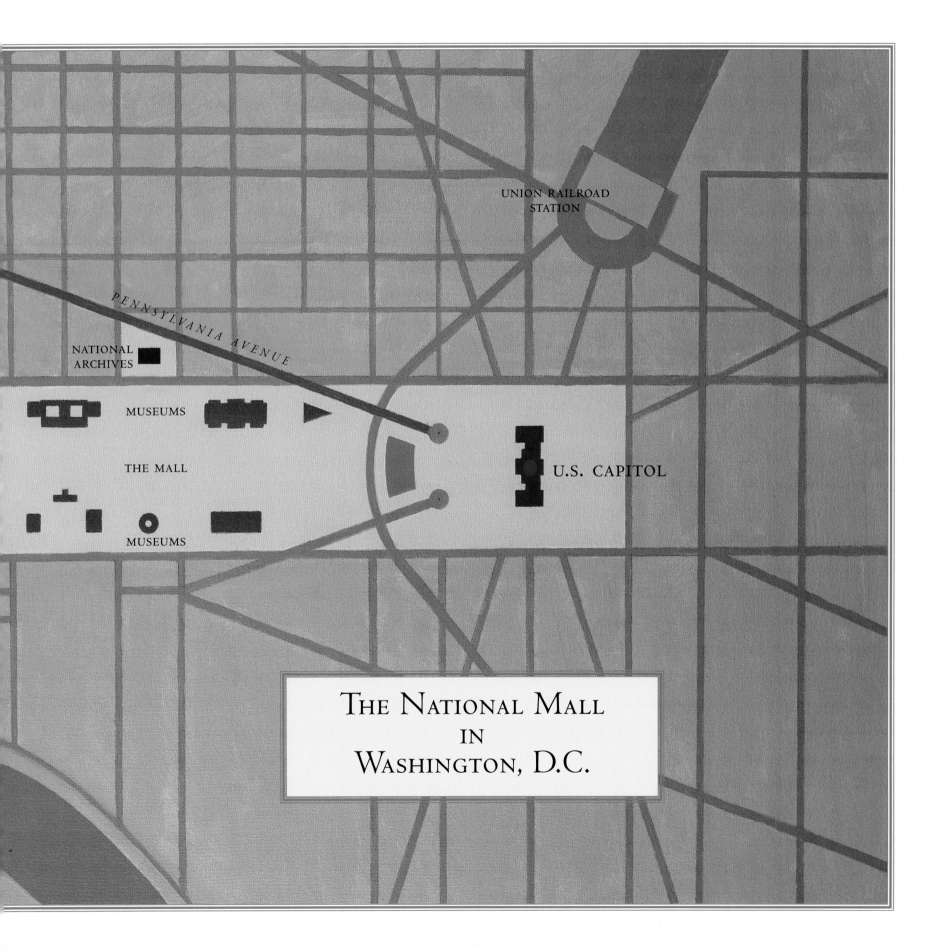

UNION RAILROAD
STATION

PENNSYLVANIA AVENUE

NATIONAL
ARCHIVES

MUSEUMS

THE MALL

U.S. CAPITOL

MUSEUMS

THE NATIONAL MALL
IN
WASHINGTON, D.C.

❧ For my parents' generation ❧

James Sherwood Curlee
1915–1986

Dorothy Anderson Curlee
1917–2002

AUTHOR'S NOTE
The word "capitol" refers to the building in which a state legislature meets.
"Capitol" refers to the building in which the U.S. Congress meets.
The word "capital" refers to the city or town serving as the seat of government.
"Capital" also means "first rate," a perfect description of our capital city!
—L. C.

BIBLIOGRAPHY
Allen, William C. *History of the United States Capitol: A Chronicle of Design, Construction, and Politics.* Washington, D.C.: Government Printing Office, 2001.
Carrier, Thomas J. *The White House, the Capitol, and the Supreme Court.* Charleston: Arcadia Publishing, 2002.
Reps, John W. *Washington On View: The Nation's Capital Since 1790.* Chapel Hill, N.C.: University of North Carolina Press, 1991.
Scott, Pamela and Antoinette J. Lee. *Buildings of the District of Columbia.* New York : Oxford University Press, 1993.
Seale, William. *The President's House: A History.* Washington, D.C.: White House Historical Association
with the cooperation of National Geographic Society, 1986.
———. *The White House: The History of an American Idea.* 2nd ed. Washington, D.C.: The White House Historical Association, 2001.
———. *The White House Garden.* Washington, DC: White House Historical Association, 1996.
Walton, William. *The Evidence of Washington.* New York: Harper and Row, 1966.
Weeks, Christopher. *Guide to the Architecture of Washington, D.C.* Baltimore: Johns Hopkins University Press, 1994.
White, George M. *Under the Capitol Dome.* Washington, D.C.: American Institute of Architects Press, 1997.

ALADDIN PAPERBACKS
An imprint of Simon & Schuster Children's Publishing Division
1230 Avenue of the Americas, New York, NY 10020
Copyright © 2003 by Lynn Curlee
ALADDIN PAPERBACKS and colophon are trademarks of Simon & Schuster, Inc.
Also available in an Atheneum Books for Young Readers hardcover edition.
Designed by Abelardo Martínez
The text of this book was set in Deepdene.
The illustrations for this book were rendered in acrylic on canvas.
Mr. Curlee would like to thank Ed Peterson for photographing the paintings.
Manufactured in China.
First Aladdin Paperbacks edition June 2006
2 4 6 8 10 9 7 5 3 1
The Library of Congress has cataloged the hardcover edition as follows:
Curlee, Lynn.
Capital / Lynn Curlee.—1st ed.
p. cm.
Summary: Provides a history of Washington, D.C., focusing on the National Mall, its monuments, and surrounding buildings.
ISBN-13: 978-0-689-84947-3 (hc.)
ISBN: 0-689-84947-8 (hc.)
[1. National monuments—Washington (D.C.)—Juvenile. 2. National monuments. 3. Washington (D.C.)—History—Juvenile literature.
4. Washington (D.C.)—Buildings, structures, etc.—Juvenile literature. 5. Washington (D.C.)—History. 6. Washington (D.C.)—Buildings, structures, etc.]
I. Title.
F194.3 C87 2002
975.3 21 2001056083
ISBN-13: 978-1-4169-1801-1 (pbk.)
ISBN-10: 1-4169-1801-9 (pbk.)